I WAS AN EMPIRE

poetry by
LYDIA GATES

ISBN: 1546842918
ISBN-13: 978-1546842910

an open letter to anyone who has asked for forgiveness

CONTENTS

I WAS AN EMPIRE

Not much is known about the ancient empire of Lydia,
which is to say I am free to create my own mythology.

Don't drink the water here,
but it's alright if you breathe the air:
just know it's salty enough to scrape you clean.
And if you thank me for it
I won't give you a welcome
because I've had to make everything, "No problem."

How did you stumble through my seaweeds,
up to my falling down outskirts of faded fabric timepiece?
Drop to your knees
for the first sign of land you've seen in days.
In the middle of my ocean
you can seek solace.

But sometimes you have to bite the hand that feeds you
and then get in return what you have given.
Take your medicine, like a mouthful of flowers;
chew them.
If you tuck them under your tongue or
into your cheek
they'll turn to poison,
the kind that is only fatal when you release
your grip on it,
try to ride the waves independent.

This is not the kind of badge of honor
you can remove from your breast

and keep breathing.
You create your best art when your fingers are functioning
in time with your head,
your Iron Age I-beams stretching to create new
    heartstrings
so you can feel gently again.

I used to feel so large
it was like hearth fire turned arson.
My own synapse citizens lit me up for the victory of taking
    me down.
An institution grows cold and leaves us little
but the barest branch of hope,
and I just want enough strength to keep building it up
    again.

Take your medicine—
like gripping the mast of a sinking ship
that may never make it back to my harbor.
You are a beating heart lighting up the darkness with each
    pulse
in this atrium.
Put it back in a body where it belongs again,
no longer strung out on my middleman.

Moor yourself to all that is left:
A hope chest of history
passed down mother to daughter to daughter again.
This is our birthright:
this smoldering ruin of timbers and thatch.
Lift your head like the hatch and climb up my rigging;
build a treehouse in the middle of skyscrapers

if you ever make it home again.

I never said we had to plant seeds
for anyone but ourselves.
Take your medicine
and take it again
and again.
Didn't you know there are consequences to breathing?
But you can call for my emergency services
when the water runs rusted,
tastes like the metal I thought about putting in my mouth,
the kind I wouldn't have been able to spit back out.

This is a collection of my architectural menagerie,
a system of metaphor and simile
held together by heathen prayer and barefoot dancing.
Anyone can live here
if only their hearts are still beating.
It's no problem;
you're welcome,
as long as you didn't expect one.
It goes down like your daily dose of medicine.

THE GOLDEN DOOR

I am the great-granddaughter of immigrants,
from the toe of the boot of Calabria,
eternally aiming its kick at Sicily.
We're the secret ingredient in our pasta sauce kinda
    people,
carried the capicola and prosciutto all the way to another
    country,
sliced it up and can I tell you about the handmade
    mozzarella, creamy and salty.

She gave birth to my grandfather in the same little town
    where he still lives,
where they've named his street after him.
From carpenter to insurance salesman to sitting village
    judge
he served his country in US Marine Corps
but never went to college, just skipped three grades.
He was the most amazing artist.
Oil paints, charcoal, crayons when I was five
soft shading, teaching me to color inside the lines,
and never letting me win at Scrabble.
He had the most amazing mind but—

Parle l'Italiano?
No, just English with an accent.
When I sang Italian happy birthday to my great-
    grandmother as she turned 100
I had learned it from a class at school, not those who were
    born with it—
not even her son could speak that poetry.

It was because his mother told him if he did
he wouldn't have been American enough,
like they didn't raise the stars and stripes every morning,
hand over hand on the rope 'til they snapped in the breeze
    and opened.
He kept it lit every night in the firefly times of summer,
humid and hungry for this dream,
of America.

I remember riding the train with him,
breathing against the window
the sharp stick of leather seats against my coffee bean
    thighs.
The air tasted like copper pennies and promises
of that better life.

I never missed a Sunday dinner or nine o'clock coffee
    time.
They didn't go to church anymore but they still lived in
    love thy neighbor style:
The doors were always open to anyone who didn't have a
    place to go,
feeding kids from three families all in the same home.
And the stories!
My father getting tricked by his sisters over and over again,
"What's a matter?" and a beciclia to the head.

I didn't get to see the New York Yankees play in person
    until after my great-grandma died,
but she had a life-sized cardboard cutout of Derek Jeter by
    her bed,
kissed him on each of her birthdays, wet smack and her

wrinkled grin.

That Grandma Francese:

She could push herself around in her wheelchair 'til the last.

She lived to 101—and a half.

Before ten you count each precious moment,

and after 100 you have to start again.

I never saw so much love inside a person,

for kids, grandkids, the greats and greats again.

She was my Mother of Exiles

and I'll carry my Lady Liberty's torch on—

Give me your tired, your poor, your huddled;

I'll bring them into my home.

NATURAL DISASTER

There are leaves missing from trees.
The New York tourists—
they take pictures of barren branches,
about to be exiled from Manhattan
for the first time in its life.

I can remember holding my own hands:
The first time I walked through city streets
unable to believe they would fall.
But sinkholes and hurricanes
have proved me wrong,
buildings burning in a downpour.

Now their bridges are underwater.
They bought so much water,
shelves barren as a black night sky,
and now it kills them,
sweeps their bodies away from the storm.

It beckoned them like the buses shutting down,
their burned-out skeletons lining the streets
above a subway that can't breathe under the ocean.
There are people tying themselves to beaches,
seaweed coiled around their ankles,
in the basements of flooded apartment buildings,
saying they're refusing to leave.

As they sit on rooftops I imagine no airplanes
flying for them, their words
daring the ground to disappear beneath them.

And then, there are some that are running.
Take refuge in the empire state building,
on the stairs leading up to the crown
of the statue of liberty.
I heard that no one is allowed there anymore.
But if you leave last,
standing alone in a jungle of empty skyscrapers,
puddles for shoes, who can stop you?

The tides pull sandbags
away from three hundred years of history,
trying to hold its breath.
For how long?
A new moon eating the city like an animal,
sustained low pressure forcing
you to exhale before you inhale
the smell of gum-printed tarmac after a storm—

I woke up from a hurricane.
I felt the static of heat lightning in my bones
and I wondered where I would be
without the smell of ozone,
without a safe place to call my own.

Nothing is left.
In my dreams:
I tried to imagine everything beautiful again, but,
I am unable to determine
what the ending of this story is
when all the bad parts are gone.

11 RESERVOIR PL

When I was asleep there were always
horns screaming
fire trucks beating
land speed records,
burning.

My hands shook instead of saved me.
In my dreams, alone,
a hungry child
painted pictures with her ashes.
I awoke pale and naked, knowing:
for ten years I was afraid of everything
and matches
haunted me like poltergeists, tripping
my life.

I carried everything I owned
in bulging bags
kept cataloged lists—
stuffed animals trailing arms,
reaching, yearning,
answering the question that still defines me:
What would you save
if your house was burning?

There are flames licking wounds
that I can no longer remember receiving.
These ties do not bind well enough,
I am unwell enough
that I cannot hide

this orange-screened sky
haunting behind my eyes.

I was a creature of habit
and peanut butter and jelly
sandwiches for most of my life.
I used to never leave the past behind,
tucking it into my bottomless bag
of ambitions clouded
by the stagnant smoke
of my burning throat,
ash covered heart until I almost
choked—

Sirens
are children screaming,
their beautiful faces asking you,
what would you save?
Me?
Me?
What about me?

In answer there is just
sweat down my
smoke, flames for everything I touch,
my fingerprints unsalvageable;
I couldn't even save myself.

In my dreams
there are never any faces.
Hate me
if I save nothing.

Hate me
if in that moment it is not a question,
but a threat, sirens
screaming.
Ashen paintings
breathing in smoke.

There is an afterimage in the fire:
the body of a child
clutching her lips.
Beside her a fallen knapsack
burning.
There is no way to escape fire lit
from your own life.

I left everything behind and
I hope you choke on that question
painted in your own misgivings,
learning:
there is nothing you can save
if your house is burning.

SUNRISE

There wasn't a day when I found out.
It wasn't an instant revelation.
Like first light before the sunrise
it came over the horizon slowly;
you looked each moment as it inched closer
until it was there,
in all of its glory.
I didn't know I could feel like that,
like I wanted to press my tongue to the sky—

I'm glad there have been millions of sunrises,
even if only twenty-four times 365
while I've been alive,
even if I've only had the chance
to see some of them.
I know that I can still can catch one, next time.

We're all told these lies about little boys
who hurt us because they love us.
But she never hurt me,
and I never loved her,
but she was the most beautiful sunrise of my life.

WRITE "SHE'S GAY" ON MY HEADSTONE

(so male historians are unable to misinterpret it)

From the first time I got my own stereo
and tuned the dial to country music radio
I never expected that kind of station to be a petitioner for
    pro-LGBT policy.
But fifteen years later when I heard someone who sounded
    a little like me
croon the words, "I've got a girl crush,"
I thought that my cowboy boots might have finally
    accepted me.

Of course, it wasn't like that.
She proceeded to ask herself the same question I once had,
but determined the opposite.
When presented with a choice to be with me,
or just be me: she chose mimicry.
It's a type of forced heteronormativity
that blinded me for years to the truth about my sexuality.

Songwriter says, "I've never heard one like that about
    jealousy."
And I replied, "That's because you're not supposed to take
    a knife
and cut the heart right out of me,
flip the script on something I thought was my beginning."

And isn't that what we have always done
take the words used against us and change them, twist the
    narrative

until it took me years to learn the truth my own history:
the color and blood of it?
I was ignorant as anyone flying a confederate flag in my
    home states
that weren't even a part of the confederacy.

We have to admit to the parts of ourselves that are less
    than savory:
I, a steak grilled and placed on the picnic table
at some redneck barbeque for them to hate at,
after I finally stopped hating myself.
And I am the kind of person who's always been allowed to
    be proud,
thankful to be able to wear this love like a badge of honor,
as long as no one had to hear someone sing about it.

The bar is set so low that I only ask
that you don't change the love song's pronouns
when you ask me to sing it,
but you mangle my words anyway.
So instead I am here to rewrite queer into every country
    song like:

That don't impress me much
because man, I feel like a woman,
and I'm not just jealous of one.
I want to be free to feel the way I feel:
Because I have a girl crush.
I will admit it to everyone,
how it's such a heart rush, lifting me up.
And I'm coming over,
but if I die young:

bury me in rainbows instead of making me one.
If I never knew the love of a man it was because
I knew the love of a woman instead,
holding my hand
and I didn't die because of it.

This is a happy ending
Even if the lyricists didn't come up with it.

CAT'S CRADLE

I'd like to think you tug on my heart strings,
because that would mean they're tied together
in a way that we can sort them back out.

Lift the loop over your soul—or thumb—
and twist me, spin me,
and turn me into something else—
a bed to a basket case
and back again.

The most important thing
is that our knots never come out,
a single loop circling itself
into figure eights of infinity.

We always played the game when we were children.
It's not just made for one person.
You pass it back and forth to someone else,
let them make your decisions
about where to step next,
let them pinch it between their fingers.

The last figure is diamonds,
and I didn't think I'd ever wear one—
but I was holding the string when we made some.

LUCY

When I was twenty-one I married a dying man.
Now, I only hold him in pictures,
and I don't cry
because you can't mourn someone who never wanted to
    be
what you imagined them.

It's been almost a year since the funeral
and I boxed up the memories he left,
pressed them into scrapbooks,
set them on the shelf as something to treasure
but never look at.
It's not a wound now,
not even a scar,
just an empty attic in my chest growing cobwebs
but I never have the energy to dust anymore.

Since that day I haven't said his name,
but in quiet corners of our own home
I can call the right one, devoid of pretenses.

Other people still think he's alive!
When the body you love doesn't host a headstone
it's easy to see why—
just a walking memory, play acting the part
the skin of your lover a freckled roadmap leading you
far away from what you thought was your home
but it's achingly familiar—
I love her.

This poem was meant to be a eulogy
but the person I love is still here.
In her smile.
In her hair.
In cats greeting you at the door when you open it.
If your body is a temple
you have to worship it.
Your lover's body *is* a temple,
and there is no wrong way to pray as long as you are doing
  it
as long as there is no ending to it.

Tell her not to accept anything less
then her own, inevitable, manifest destiny
where she takes up all the space she deserves.
Put her on a pedestal but don't blame her when she falls,
just pick her up again.

When she rises from that grave other people built for him,
same face, different expression—
it's not a miracle.
It's not because you loved her.
It's because she was able to love herself,
no more or less than anyone else does.

This was supposed to be a eulogy,
but instead it's just a whispered breath in my lover's ear
telling her that she is real,
unapologetically, standing here.

It is spring.
The flowers bloom on the only land she's ever owned,

her gravestone,
but she's ready to sell it.

These months are a time for cleaning
so, we leave the past behind together,
opening up our windows—
and I sweep out my ribcage.
I never realized just how much love was in there.

I'll climb to the top of the hill and sing it,
even if I sound like a bird on its first wing
screaming among the leaves
and then catching the breeze,
so shocked in my own fortune that I fall
and roll, and roll.
And I'm dizzy on the side of the hill,
sneezing in the flowers, looking up at clouds.

There are no shapes that look like anything I recognize
from the fraction of life I've been alive.
It reminds me that when you stare up to that blue sky
if you were just to look far enough you'd see everything,
and you're so small
but you're still the most important thing to someone.

I take the scrapbook off the shelf,
open it and show her what I remember,
and then add more to it
each time I'm convinced it's the end.

SOLSTICE

I used to work nights; sleep during the daytime.
I didn't miss the sunshine, but now I love it.
Except for those weeks when we're parted like equinoxes,
pass each other with fingers brushing
because we each have our own equal amounts of time.

We spend evening separated by headphones and
    paperbacks,
and the cracks in a scoliosis spine.
It's the proximity to each other we crave,
like a constellation, each star alone for billions of miles,
but that's almost nothing in the space of our sky tonight.

For two hours you roll into bed with me,
crash into a pillow like the waves pull the moon.
And then we reach out to each other,
even though you're the type that doesn't cuddle.

When I wake we are tangled like the red string in my
    pocket,
not sure how it got there, sticky and knotted:
like our morning hair and lips.

It's unexpected like a cloud over the moon
those moments I can reach out and touch you,
feel nothing but the pulse through our temporary veins
until the seasons change.

DEATH & GIRLS

I knew there were things I was never supposed to love
like death,
and girls.

Last year my New Year's resolution was to go to therapy.
I had never been,
because the last time I had spoken to a mental health
    professional
I was only nineteen and crying in the student union
    bathroom.
"Are you having thoughts of suicide?" they asked.
"Are you a danger to yourself?"
And I told them honestly that I didn't really want to die—
I just wanted to be dead.

Instead of offering a temporary solution
to my permanent problem, they said:
The only crisis you're allowed to have
is a knife to your wrist
or a gun to your head
and if you're swallowing that poison past your lips
there's a place for you,
but if you just never want to get up again—
there's an appointment, three months away
see if you can hold on to that rope long enough
for us to pull you up, or if you'll give in
and hang yourself with it.

I was the lie of the bystander effect
at the side of my own bed.

Surely someone else would call 911 if I deserved it,
because Kitty Genovese was just misrepresented by the
    media,
so, when you Google her all you get is her funeral,
how she was untouchable,
not the life of a queer Italian woman in 1960's America,
not how she was held as she was bleeding, hot copper
not the two people who called for help to come,
3 AM the lights—
cool blue and warm, blood red.

But that's not the kind of thing that's good enough
to be commercially collectible pain,
the poster girl on tabloids
the subject of our tragic study—
And just like that, I'm back to therapy.

I told him:
I'm not here to romance suicide;
I fucking knew it would get better
And I don't want people to say:
"If you google her, all you'll get is her funeral."
Not the life of a queer Italian woman in 2017 America,
whose body is no longer that untouchable exclusion zone,
who keeps her resolutions—

I like to think I'm better now.
But I know there are some things you cannot change,
like loving death,
and loving girls.

SOUTHWEST SCARS

You could say I had "Valley Fever,"
or at least the desire to be as far away from "home" as I
   could be.
I ran all the way across the country,
like I was a steer and the cowboys were after me.
This is really my wild west
and I still get excited every time I see a tumbleweed

I made my first love here:
landed in a barren stretch of sand,
breathed in its dust and—
I can say this is the place that I really grew up,
like that scrubbed up weed, rolling
until I was holding the sides of those northern peaks
and growing.

My best friend was what people thought of
when they whispered "Arizona,"
brown leather boots and big girl guns
stomping through the mud to her 2500 truck,
taking me to hug my first cactus
just as the sun came up.
Her skin was just the right gold-kissed tan
and her shorts were never short enough.

But up here it's only truly hot a few days in the summer,
so, we went down to the desert like its lover—
if only it didn't happen so fast,
I would have had the chance to do more
than just touch her.

But that valley never meant to give me up.
I can survive record high temperatures
swatting flies, toasting my heels over bonfires.
When the blue skies gave the desert its goodnight
we were there, two sides of a best friendship locket
falling asleep in the dust.

I never felt pain like I was supposed to.
Roll 'em on back to years when I ignored the things that
    hurt too much.
I lost my Arizona girl being so tired every morning
that I just couldn't keep up.
She left me home and went alone
to see the sunrise over the Grand Canyon;
I was too busy itching away my skin
fighting to breathe as the dunes were closing in.

Three different doctors diagnosed me with something,
and all of them were wrong.
It felt like the time we got tan so fast it all peeled off,
like it never even happened.
Now that's how I feel about her, sometimes,
like there are moments when she never touched my life
but that's a lie.

I still have the scars to prove that I left her,
my valley fever burned down to embers
but I still stoke the coals sometimes in the night.
I forgive her.

Remember:

A beautiful girl with her boots all over mud
she takes my hand and holds it up
we're screaming to the radio
and painting up the town,
but now, she's become "a good friend of mine."
So, I'll never have to tell you her name.
So, I'll never give in to the trauma of our endings.
So, I'll just tell you the good memories we made, along the
    way.

CLOUDY WITH A CHANCE

She talks about her love like the forecast:
Things are bound to clear up by the weekend.
But if there's one thing I know about meteorologists
it's that they're all too often misguided,
seeing what they want to see in storm fronts
or text messages.

Look at how many minutes it took him to reply.
Now double it.
She says, this is the science behind him always wanting
     you;
there's a high chance of sunshine.

But the clouds roll in unexpected
the exponential growth of thunderheads, until
the terrifying "K"
of a lightning strike.

She's talking to three different people,
intersecting cold fronts of fuck boys.
Sometimes she doesn't hear from any of them,
spending the weekend inside
waiting for the rain to end.
And sometimes it's a heat wave of hair curlers
destroying the whole ozone layer so more sun can hit her
     skin—

There's a little place I come from
where we call rain in that time a sun shower.
It's so beautiful it breeds rainbows,

and that's the boy she finally takes home
to watch it from her window.
I hope she doesn't check the forecast anymore.

POLYGONS

On loving two women at the same time:

First of all, get them to know each other.
They both hold a part of your heart or
the whole thing, equally, each with a hand.
You have two hands for holding,
two eyes for seeing for seeing their beauty
as you bend both of your knees at the altar of their lips.
They don't even need to like each other,
but it would be great if they did.

Especially because there are a lot of board games
you need three or more people to play
and it's easier to remember where you lost your keys
when there's more people who might have seen you put
   them away.

Second: do not feel the need to justify yourself.
Do not feel the need to explain yourself.
You are not the slut you were named.
What is a slut, anyway?
Just another person because
I posit that everyone's got to live their life
in some kind of way
and they don't all need to be the same.

So, instructionally, I have to say:
Have lots of sex with everyone you love—
have more than one but less than infinite lovers.
Give of yourself and get everything back, multiplied.

Reject serial monogamy, those closed hearts in revolving
    doors,
instead your love is open.

Third: do not believe in soul mates.
How can you expect to find your one in seven billion in
    your backyard?
Especially when, honestly, a state is basically a backyard,
at least when you consider the number of people
    overpopulating this planet
and the human mind's inability to calculate simple addition
    on its own.
Addition like: one plus one equals... I don't know.
It doesn't feel like there are enough numbers in that
    equation.

Basically, what I'm saying is,
when you take a number like seven billion and divide it
in hetero-monogamous half, honestly
you can't conceptualize the difference besides
your learned knowledge that seven is bigger than three
    point five,
and you never thought even just one person would love
    you.

Fourth: is your love still open?
You have to take it by the reins and own it.
The distance between people is communication;
give an explanation.
Tell your lover why you love them!
I know, it sounds simple, but people like you and me need
    validation.

On that topic,
don't expect to get everything from one person.
Expect to build your life out of Lego blocks, each a
    different color,
each a different door to open,
hundreds of possibilities if you get to know them.

Fifth: remember what I said about sluts and soul mates?
Well, they are what you make them.
Create them.
You can call your lover whatever you want.
Personally, I only know how to love people
    unconditionally.
It hurts sometimes, but otherwise,
it's a beautiful moon in the dark parts of my sky,
and boy is it nice, when there are two moons orbiting this
    home planet I call my body,
lit by the red giant star-sun of my too big love,
reaching out to the restaurant at the end of the universe.

The great thing about planetary metaphors
is that, for all intents and purposes,
they're always going to be there.
We live this short life and,
regardless of how many times the heat death threatened,
I'm glad that my world is still spinning.
I get down on both my knees. Rock me.
Love is not the fragile thing we imagined it to be.

ARABESQUE

I didn't want to grow tall.
I wanted to keep myself compact
so I would always be small enough
to fit into other people's costumes,
wear their tutus,
be the prima ballerina dollhouse fairy girl,
bind my feet with silk and resin
to dance Coppélia, or sugarplums.

Instead I always had to be Arabian,
wasn't blonde or small enough for their auditions,
so, I flipped it—
stepped high on my tip toes.
But I was a kind of middle child,
the moral of the proverb.
You don't realize the meaning 'til it's over,
'til my tights showed tattoos
'til my hands threw punches
at everyone who told me I wasn't:
Tall enough
Skinny enough
just plain Enough.

If I were a giant I could crush them.
But instead I'd run away to make the stage
my reading nook,
enveloped by velvet curtains,
everything but hidden
in the last place they'd think to look.

VANITY SIZED

You're not supposed to ask women about their weight!

But when it comes to me people seem to think it's a game.
You're skinny, surely, you couldn't take it the wrong way.
Well, to avoid any confusion about whether or not I'd like
    to play...
I'll tell you: I weigh 110 pounds on a good day,
and at five feet six that means I am underweight.

The last time I went to the doctor he felt the need to ask
    me:
How is your relationship—
with food?
It's just a question we have to ask people like you
who might carry extra quarters in their pockets,
a tactic I'm intimately familiar with
after years seeing girls hug toilets to be tutu pretty,
looking at me with jealousy
because I could still eat.

But I couldn't go to the bathroom in restaurants
after someone suspected me bulimic.
Liddi, you're so, so skinny—
So why the fuck is this dress a medium?

They teach you to aspire to the smallest size,
an impossibility you couldn't fit a ribcage in,
even when it's poking out so you can count them.
I'd like to tell you my final rib sticks out genetically.

My legs are long and lean
but too muscular for the right size skinny jeans.
I don't have a thigh gap,
but if I stick out my butt it looks like it.
I do that sometimes;
Fat girls aren't the only ones who can't see themselves in
    magazines;
when I'm naked
I don't look like a magazine.

In pushback, there are companies
that have vanity sized me off their scale,
made my mother's ten a two
and my two a negative irrationality,
the square root sign over my body
reminding us that numbers don't matter that much—
because effectively they mean nothing in reality.

People have told me they'd love me more if there was
    more of me,
but there's beauty in the less of me:
how I chew off my hangnails
digesting them so nothing is lost
consuming myself slowly,
a self-sufficient system that doesn't need them for
    anything.

And I'm seeing myself in their funhouse mirrors
of the same numbered size,
trying to find the exit sign,
trapped in their dressing rooms.
And I shouldn't run with scissors

but I am using them to cut these misfit clothes off
then run away from you.

And I like the way I look!
I stare at myself in every reflective surface.
Beauty
is in the eye of the industry
but I want to take it back.
Name all the measurements lovely
and label them accessibly.
Don't resize me so I feel pretty,
just make the clothes to fit me.

Oh, and pockets?
I like that shit.

SKINNY

I used to be skinny.
Not that I am not skinny now,
but I was Skinny, as in that was my name.
Hello, my name is Skinny.
Call me another but it won't be the same.

My father said if I turned sideways I would disappear,
as if my body was two-dimensional in a 3D world.
I didn't take up space.
I walked into a room and no one noticed me.
You can't have vocal cords without room to vibrate,
so, instead of speaking,
I ate & ate, but I never gained weight.

Who belongs to these toothpick arms on a pencil body,
paper-thin hands bringing food to her lips?
It's Skinny.
Other girls wanted to be me—
even if they couldn't see me—
but I was just happy I was healthy,
even if you always tried to fatten me up.
I found the existential plane where I could rip off my
    name.
Trust me, I've eaten enough.

CENTENO

Teenagers scare the living shit out of me
they could care less unless someone—
will teach them.
You don't need a degree to give that to them,
just a pine board knotted between your knuckles,
the ones toughened over and over with microfractures
until they're no longer matchsticks
but musical instruments
tapping a tattoo to your heartbeat.

It was about discipline.
We learned how to hurt someone
but the sticking point wasn't who
just why and when
and sure, it was self-defense against physical threats,
but the most important thing to remember
was the war waging inside of them.
Because teenagers are a car crash you just can't stop
   looking at
an invincibility complex that always makes it out alive
until it doesn't.

I was there too, sixteen and green dressed in black:
my belt tied a little too tightly,
tucked, because it hung a little too long.
How was I supposed to claim to be Sensei,
teach them the steps in a dance I had only barely
   "mastered"
so they could follow along?

It was about balance.
Stand in your stirrups and rein them in
but sometimes give them their head
and tell them to sprint.
Be strong, be strict,
but above all be forgiving
of mistakes and outtakes
and a fist to your chin.

Thanks to them
I wasn't made of glass anymore,
once a ballerina show piece pretending to fit in,
no, I had brought some grace but really
my place was bare feet on mats
and a different kind of kicking,
spinning, tripping,
my ankles out from under me like falling fawns
but we almost all made it to the end of spring.

I've always wanted to be a teacher.
From the first time I learned that teaching one thing
was really teaching that and something else
to those whose knuckles passed through me like smoke,
from the burning half of the house of their head.
Build it again and again, and again,
remaking themselves each time they stepped into my dojo
its own house when they didn't have one.

It's about perspective.
People called them bad kids,
but we didn't.
We picked up the pieces of their accidents,

dredged up their oil spills,
and now sometimes I still see them:
their hands wrapped tight around life's steering wheel.

SPECTRUM

My name is five letters long but even so
it is exactly half vowels
(you know, and sometimes Y).
In addition, there's the symmetry of five
letters in each of my names,
and you might suggest my satisfaction with these
   commonalities
means I have OCD,
but really,
that illness is a lot less common than you think it to be.

But you're convinced there's something wrong with me.
That twitch in my hand,
the fidget in my feet,
it must be anxiety.
You have an herbal remedy,
a series of breathing exercises,
anything to make me breathe;
you're remembering to breathe, right?
(breathe)

You ask:
Why don't you look me in the eyes?
Did it really take you three years to realize
your lover's were green brown gold?
How didn't she leave you if you were too broken to look
   at her
doesn't she need someone to hold?
You don't let anyone touch.
Over-sensitized, and you feel too much.

Hold her face in your hands and look on repeat.
Repeat.

Repeat yourself I didn't hear you.
Really, I mean there's a disconnect in my head—
your words did actually go in one ear
but never came out the other
they went missing somewhere,
never got up on the right side of the bed.
Can you repeat the question?
Repeat.
Repeat.

Can you describe the perpetrator
at the scene of your crimes?
She's about five feet five,
long brown hair, dark brown eyes,
once weighed as little as 105,
could run between the raindrops,
didn't care about the color of the sky,
looked herself in the mirror,
couldn't see it any clearer—
because other people had labeled her broken.
They never taught her the rules that went socially
    unspoken.

Now she says:
Tell me if I'm being obnoxious.
I know I'm a little bit toxic.
Please don't blame me for my repeated responses.
Please don't blame me for my repeated responses.

I'm not reading off this script from disinterest.
I wrote three to give you variety,
running them over and over in my head on repeat.
Repeat.
Every night as I'm falling asleep,
I'm imagining that you just might talk to me.
I'm clinging to anyone a little bit friendly.
I'm sorry,
so sorry.

Eventually,
or after five minutes if you're still listening to
something about my cats
or the books that I read
I'll tell you, jokingly:
At the age of three
after a doctor told my parents and they never told me
I got labeled an "Aspie."
The apple that fell too far from the tree.
But even after being hidden under the rug
I kinda like who I turned out to be.
Fuck whatever you call "normalcy."

DOCTOR FRANKENSTEIN

Your strongest sensory memory is smell.
It can take you back in an instant—
like a lightning strike.
They say lightning never strikes the same place twice
but it has struck my body hundreds,
maybe even thousands, of times,
each memory lighting me up like—

Do you know lightning smells the way burnt supper tastes?
I can't cook because I don't want to go back to that place.
Sawdust summers and asphalt littered with cicada skins,
bright outside but my father worked nights—
Which is to say, I lived in darkness.

I can see the place where it entered my skin
cracked me open with spider web scars
to become the blood of the body I lived in,
branching out like trees through capillaries and
maybe I can grow through it, but:
Can you run when you're powered entirely by lightning?
Every time you count to five
thunder rumbles and you can't remember anything.

Poison ivy has no discernable smell,
but I remember we're both immune to it
unless it gets under our skin—
Like I let you get under my skin;
I should have been immune to you but
I talked back when I knew you were wrong,
mostly associated you with that slamming door

and its implication of poison—
I mean lightning—

I like to think it was a thunderstorm,
rain spinning down in sheets
to hide a guardrail in the dark—
Instead of you, the drunk driver
on your way home from the bar.

It's not like you can remember what happened anyway
after they cobbled you back together
out of your own damaged parts.
Frankenstein was laid out on that table and shocked
to become his own monster,
who got a redemption arc.

They say each of your cells renews at least once every
    seven years.
Gives you a new body.
It's been at least that long so why can I still see
the exit wound you left on me?
It's a bullet as large as the elephant in this living room,
Reminding me that I can't just forget
But also need to work on forgiving.

How do you forgive someone for crimes they don't
    remember committing?

The same way you forgive the thunderstorm your shiver,
the poison ivy your rash,
the darkness your isolation,
the door your flinch as a ghost slams it shut,

the gun your triggers,
the smell of burning your memory—
You do it by saying, "I love you," to someone
who was once your enemy.

TEST DRIVE

Become a perfect driver in ten hours or less!
That is to say, conform to the expectations
set before you at the age of sixteen,
now one-third of your lifetime ago.
All this for the low, low price of $500
or another refill of Lexapro.

Upon meeting the driving instructor:
Excuse the heart from inside your throat,
the cracks from between your knuckles,
and don't let him know that last night
you had a nightmare
of running a red light right into your own body,
and peeling back your skin to do unscheduled
maintenance.

The car rumbles to life under your fingers:
4 cylinders of—after 3 weeks of—
you can name all the parts of the engine—the brain—
understand how they intertwine—
the neural pathways—
but as soon as you put your foot on the—
open your mouth and—
the wrong things always spill out
like leaking antifreeze
poisonous to those who consume it.

Keep an emergency toolkit in your trunk;
get your oil changed every 3,000
negative thoughts,

hand over your credit card for $80 of coping mechanisms
when your engine combusts.

At the used car dealership:
the fresh paint is barely dry
but the title is salvage;
the transmission only has one gear
and you're stuck in reverse.
Don't bother to get behind the wheel.

The good thing is:
there is always another car.
People trade in everything about themselves,
dealership lots like psychologist's lobbies,
telling them what they need
but you didn't bring your past today
to lien against this loan.

When your hands are shaking at ten & two
on your test drive—un-medicated,
there is no instructor knocking you back against your seat,
no emergency brake
in your life, anymore.
You're left asking yourself
who is watching,
failing to understand that finally
you're in charge of yourself.

And you buy that car—
Kind of used and needs some work
but you've always been a fixer upper
and those make the most on return.

HOLY GROUND

I used to think God was in dust motes.
To me there was nothing more spiritual
than a stripe of sunlight through the window
illuminating the invisible.
Churches were holy places
inspiring my wonder to believe—

But it got a little more complicated
when I had to eat the body and drink of his son:
I thought Jesus just turned water into wine,
not the blood of my covenant,
always thicker than the water of my womb.
Aren't the most important things what you get to choose?

I've always been one to look for answers.
I couldn't settle for predestination—
it must all be explained through meditation!
Travel all the way around the world
just to settle my skepticism.

But karma is only a great concept for the pious,
A little less so for those of us who tripped on a root,
fell down the rabbit hole
and ended up in Wonderland.
It's hard to make decisions
when there's smoke clouding your vision
And I'm not sure judgment on the turn of the wheel
is really any different.

Good thing they sells books on magic

right in the middle of Wal-Mart!
There's something to be said for instant gratification.
In addition to offering a feminine deity
there's also the power to drink the blood of your enemies.
Or wait, isn't that Satanic?
No, and it turns out the instructions harm no one,
like what you expected the commandments to be.
Light a candle, raise the athame, and just breathe.
They burned witches because they thought we weren't
    nice,
but we're only burning incense tonight.

I joined a coven of my own creation,
tried to heal,
because you can't let hate
be the only flame in your whole life.

Get yourself a familiar:
A black cat, bright green eyes.
He's your conscience, but the flip side.
Don't worry who tries to tell you
what box you fit in
because you can just ask the cat—
it's very different, the one
you put yourself inside.

Worship the moon.
Worship your mother.
Worship the purple soles of your feet
stomping through fallen mulberries beneath the trees.
Really, I guess you just need to worship something,
spiritually.

What would you do without the links of a leash
hands holding tight over your lips
while you wait for the commands:
roll over, sit up, *speak.*

Now, I tell everything like jokes:
A Ouija board and a Tarot deck
will walk into a bar.
I know, because my tea leaves told me.
They were also there in the past, surely,
and now it's the present, some kind of gift—
because I don't think anything happens when you die.
You're just in the ground, buried, or burned on the breeze.
So why don't you make your life the best heaven it can be
and go on, live the hell out of it.

LOVE STORIES

Lucy, I'm home!
Ricky Ricardo enters stage left,
takes off his coat, and embraces his wife.
She looks over his shoulder,
hair curled and eye sparkling.
He's the love of her life.

Let me tell you a story:
My grandfather was a slicked-back Marine
and my grandmother a golden-haired queen.
When my father was born
his father became a carpenter
so they could build memories with
big Italian gestures and wooden spoons,
Pall Malls between brown fingers,
and red lipstick pressed to cheeks.
It's been 65 years and they're still living that dream,
making new memories to replace the ones he's lost.
He's still the love of her life.

In another story:
My mother's mother's headstone reads Joan V Love.
I'm not sure if the V should stand for
one of her 43 ex-lover's names or
vengeance for all the wrongs they made.
Rough slaps across the cheek in the middle of the night,
running only to cling to the first man she could find.
I don't think I have to spell it out:
she never found the love of her life.

When those stories collide:
My mother was folded tight like origami.
How couldn't she run to lights that came down
in a psychedelic sunset,
chords so loud they couldn't hear anything as they
  screamed?
When he first saw her: she was bathed in a hot blue glow
like the suit he wore to their wedding.

How do you tame that soul? No.
How do you tame love so bright it's a firework:
Sizzle. Crack. Across the sky—
Until it goes.
You have to hold that memory,
wear it smooth like the inside of a shell.
Like how her heart got hollow:
love falling through the cracks in their foundation—
depreciation of his sun, and moon, and stars.
The honeymoon was over:
She was the love of his life
but he wasn't hers.

In my story:
I didn't know what I was looking for.
I manufactured crushes on band geeks with bangs
and laughed the one girl who asked me out away.
One summer I found a pretty boy with hazel eyes,
picked out of the sky like an apple.
I bit into him, and let our memories grow,
thinking if something went wrong at least I would know.

She hasn't cut her hair in over two years now,

trying to become what she sees inside herself.
I tell her she's beautiful every day.
Neither of us are what we were expected to be but:
I open the door.
I take off my coat.
I embrace my wife and I whisper:
Lucy, I'm home!
This is the love I'll have for the rest of my life.

CREATION MYTH

It's common not to know the circumstances of your own birth. Memories of the event are built from other people's recollections told so many times one begins to tell them oneself. There are pictures painted for me of a baby swaddled pink and the horn-rimmed glasses on her face. Regardless, there are some things I do know for sure. I was her first child, even though it had been a long time since she married that man I've come to call my father. I know that I came into the world with tan skin and a mess of curly black hair. I know my real name.

Birth is supposed to be a hard thing, but it's said I slipped out so fast the doctor didn't even see me coming, didn't have his gloves on, could have missed the party. You know, you're not supposed to eat anything at the party, but it's said I drank from her breasts. Or was it someone like me, who was put there for jealousy to steal the twinkling spark of my brown eyes? I don't doubt I looked for circles of flowers as soon as I could walk, stumbled under a hill and spent years there before I got out.

You know, they say you should put out milk and bread for the fairies. Like children they thrive on the nutrition our own bodies and hands create for us. But the milk is only a taste of what they could have had. And the bread? It's full of seeds and other lies; it's nothing like flesh. Their teeth are sharp and meant for ripping, how could you insult them like that? Maybe my mother forgot to hang a horseshoe above the door or, more likely, hung it upside down; what I'm saying is I'm a little crooked, now.

No one could ever decide who she looked like, one of my father's two faces or my mother's heart. Isn't it a tenet of the fairies that they metamorphosize? Take on and slip out of glamour, always giving you what you want. She tried to be a good child. But good children don't talk back, don't ask questions, only speak when they are spoken to, don't make some much goddamn noise; she learned to be small, sometimes. Didn't meet anyone's eyes. She was light enough to lift herself up on fairy wings and, because she didn't want her feet to touch the ground, she picked her heels up to experience less of it. She didn't want the socks to touch her so she pulled them apart at the seams and left them under my bed like a distorted self-portrait, so she walked around on bare feet.

Something just wasn't right about her. People suspected she was a puzzle with a missing piece, whispered behind their fingers at family gatherings. She didn't line up pretty with the cousins, was too tall or too skinny. I couldn't even make friends with the ones I had built in. The suspicion faded eventually but it had gone on long enough that for a while, I even suspected myself.

Between the two of us I remember things as they weren't. I stepped into another world at the age of ten and had to learn everything for the first time, but also all over again. I was missing all the rules even when I sat in the front of the class. I had to fight for each interaction, but is it really your fight if you don't know why you are fighting it? I liked to ask questions. I missed the place where she had gone back.

Fairies can't tell lies, I remind myself. But they can twist the truth. I couldn't tell lies, I remind myself; someone always saw right through. I sat in class and they told me to recall my most embarrassing moment, but I didn't know how that felt. I sat in class and they told me to tell a story of the summer, but I couldn't pick the real from my fantasy. I sat in class and they told me to write a cartoon, make it funny. I couldn't tell jokes. I could only make up magical worlds if they were really things that happened to me, or her, in my memories, I mean fantasies. It's a good thing your mind twists what you remember; each time you rethink it you remake it.

I learned my own kind of glamour. I lifted the corners of my lips because that's supposed to mean you're happy. I stored everything I heard so I could repeat it in the right moment, where it fit in the script. I laughed when everyone else laughed, even if I didn't find it funny, hoping it would sound genuine. I learned to fit in, but I withered away a little at a time, wasting away on the inside instead of the outside like those poor children buried in the coals for the sin of being swapped for something almost like their kin.

A mother could plead insanity at the death of me, and many did, but my mother told me to love my monster. I thought she meant my father, but now I wonder if she knew I was a myth, a folktale, a child destined to have a twofold nature, one side real the other painted on, each year more skillfully. There are a lot of stories where the monster isn't what you expected it to be, secretly someone friendly, secretly it was the realest parts of me.

She raised me as her own even when someone else would have cooked dinner in eggshells to scare me into speech. She apologized for my father after I was grown and she learned of his sharp teeth. They matched her mother's sharp sewing scissors she had thought would protect me, but he used them to switch me. They switched me. Someone switched me. I asked for a fairy godmother but I already had one, myself my own sister, a changeling, I miss her. I've lost who I was supposed to be, only seen in stolen moments, a faded photograph of a girl running through a forest to a circle of fairy trees.

STAR SIGNS

The river is planets lit along another kind of way,
like the whiskey one we never let past our lips,
painting petroglyphs with how hard we kissed.

A billion miles away it would be the same:
an intergalactic continuum of hands on hips defiance,
trying to find each other in the middle of this wilderness,
where there is always enough of each other to sip.

This babbling brook doesn't say any words
that I know how to miss.
There's just you, and not the sound of it.

I turn from of a waterfall of galaxies into the past,
because time is only passing in one
of our infinite parallel instances
and in all else we are here, in each encapsulated moment.

I hold it in my mind as a prize
with the time to carve us into the dark of it.

Do you know how much nothing there is in space?
How much there is here inside of us,
whose atoms can never really touch,
each of us so far apart even from ourselves?

We never got to the point where I could look you in the
    eyes;
we needed more time,
forgetting that is what we had more than anything.

If only we could swim for it—
don't stop to read the petroglyphs,
because we can be ancient enough come before them
and after they're gone
we are still slipping through space.

CONSTELLATIONS

I used to catch fireflies in mason jars.
The nights are still dark now,
but lit with a different kind of twinkling star,
nothing so close as those
cloud blanketed keep the heat in summer nights,
holding the sunset's light
as the mosquitoes came out to bite—

Me with my glass prison,
for the only hope I could see:
Lightning bugs.
They'll die if you take them inside,
their black bodies shriveled up by morning.
You can only keep them in the liminal space
of a northeast backyard,
the sweat trickling down your ribs in the darkness,
each blink of them lighting up a different part of you,
but never showing the whole picture.

They're as far away as stars now.
It would take lifetimes for that light to reach me again,
but I still think about them,
wave my hand across the sky,
close my eyes and open
to see the fragility of those winking lights.

How many times before it's sunrise?

ACKNOWLEDGEMENTS

Juniper House Readings for the simultaneous publication of the poem "I Was an Empire," the prompts that inspired it, "Arabesque," "Star Signs," and "Sunrise," and a generous and welcoming community.

Flagstaff Poetry Slam and Sedona Poetry Slam for the space to get my words out and the ever-present support.

My Chemical Romance for the first lines of "Centeno."

My family and the friends that are part of it, for everything.

ABOUT THE AUTHOR

Lydia Gates is a cat mother, a reader of all things fantasy, and keeper of the purple pens. Her first loves are good food and uninterrupted sleep, but she resides in mostly sunny Flagstaff, AZ with her second one. She is a member of the 2017 Sedona Poetry Slam NPS team.

contact: lydiajeangates@gmail.com